Han Tümertekin Recent Work

Edited by Hashim Sarkis

with Neyran Turan and Rengin Toros

ISBN 0-935617-91-4

Book and cover design by
Wilcox Design, Cambridge, MA

The Harvard University Graduate
School of Design is a leading center
for education, information, and
technical expertise on the built
environment. Its departments of
Architecture, Landscape
Architecture, and Urban Planning
and Design offer masters and doctoral degree programs and provide
the foundation for its Advanced
Studies and Executive Education
programs.

Preface and Acknowledgments

This publication is the outcome of the Aga Khan Public Lecture that Han Tümertekin delivered at the Harvard University Graduate School of Design on April 23, 2005. The yearly event is meant to bring to Harvard a talented designer from the Middle East and Muslim world and to further expose the designer's work through a publication.

I would like to gratefully acknowledge the sponsorship of the Aga Khan Trust for Culture and the Harvard University Graduate School of Design. The ongoing collaboration of the Harvard University Press as distributors of the Aga Khan book series is also appreciated.

For their help in putting together this volume, I would like to thank Melissa Vaughn, Director of Publications and Exhibitions at the GSD; book designer Jean Wilcox; Rengin Toros from Han Tümertekin's office in Istanbul; Neyran Turan, the Aga Khan publications coordinator at the GSD; administrative coordinator Maria Moran; Pars Kibarer; and Gülçin Becerik.

TÜMERTEKİN, THE STRANGER *Hashim Sarkis*

The Ninth Triannual Cycle of the Aga Khan Award for Architecture honored seven projects for their unique contributions to design culture throughout the Muslim world: the Petronas Towers in Kuala Lumpur, the new library of Alexandria, a primary school in Burkina Faso, a revitalization project in the Old City of Jerusalem, the restoration of a mosque in Yemen, the Sandbag Shelter Prototype project, used for various emergency situations, and the B2 House in Çanakkale, Turkey, by Han Tümertekin. The jury that included internationally renowned architects, artists, and philosophers chose a broad array of projects that addressed an equally extensive range of cultural and social concerns. The pluralism of the architecture of the Islamic world and the diversity of its cultures were vividly represented and celebrated in this selection of projects for the year 2004.

When compared with previous award winners, the honored designs fit quite comfortably within familiar project types: the community-oriented urban rehabilitation project, the pilot restoration project, the social agent, and the icon building. Although by no means fully inclusive of all award recipients, these categories do reveal the convergence of design and social values highlighted by the award over time and the types of projects that tend to convey these values most eloquently.

If examined through this lens of Aga Khan Award categorization, the B2 House could readily fit in yet another regular award-winning category, the Turkish villa. Over its nine cycles, the Aga Khan Award has identified several houses, built for the most part in the Turkish countryside, as in vitro experiments in how contemporary architecture could interact with different vernaculars. Yet upon further examination, what must have stood out as cultural references to successive juries—from Sedat Hakkı Eldem's appropriations of Anatolian motifs toward a national architecture, to Nail Çakırhan's readmittance of Ottoman references to the national canon, to Turgut Cansever's Bodrum houses that reconcile Turkish architecture with Byzantine tectonics and Sedat Gürel's reconciliation with Aegean typologies—radically differ from the B2 House.[1] When it comes to vernacular references, Tümertekin's project sits on the fence.

The house is a small, two-story box made of a free-spanning concrete frame. Stone infill inside the frame wraps the exterior walls as well as the roof, employing stone as a peculiar though not unprecedented roofing material. The bamboo screen inside the thin metal frame of the shutters contrasts with the heaviness of the frame. The weight of the box is also countered by the disengaged way it sits on the stone fence. It refuses the choice of being grounded in the landscape or floating above it. It avoids the choice not only because it is built from a different material from that of the wall it sits on, but because it refuses to commit to any position about regionalism, iconography, or site—matters that have tormented Tümertekin's Turkish predecessors and, more generally, many architects in the developing world. In the postcolonial Third World, any serious architectural output has always been interpreted as a local response to a generic Western modernism. In that sense, many developing-world architects have gone down the slippery slope of believing in such a dichotomy, reducing their architectures to an expression of a predetermined debate.

In the context of this award cycle, and as a ground for isolated but intense formal exploration, the B2 House stood alone among the 2004 awards for its sheer architectural statement. Perhaps with the exception of the Lepers' Hospital in Chopda Taluka, India, by Per Christian Brynildsen and Jans Olaf Jensen, few projects in the history of the award are noteworthy for their intense formal exploration and are not overwhelmed by their social or contextual aspects.

This refusal to be grounded could be explained by the fact that the house belongs to two frequent travelers—"two urban nomads," as Tümertekin describes them. Such cosmopolitan travelers thrive on their ability to transgress context and to remain strangers, even at home. This stance may also be explained through a shift in attitude among a new generation of Turkish architects in general and in Tümertekin's work in particular, characterized by a strategic disengagement from the architectural debates in Turkey yet countered by an open dialogue with larger disciplinary discussions today and by a full immersion in the particulars of practice in Turkey. This reshuffling of priorities merits further examination.

The disengagement from the Turkish context is not immediately obvious, for Tümertekin is very much at home in Istanbul. Born and raised there, he studied at the Istanbul Technical University, one of the oldest and most vigorous platforms of architectural and urban debate in the Middle East. After working for two years in the office of Ahmet Gülgönen, a key figure in Turkish architecture, he established a partnership with another Turkish architect, Reşit Soley, and set up his own practice, Mimarlar Tasarım Danışmanlık, in Istanbul. Recognition from within the Turkish establishment has come early. He has twice been awarded Turkey's National Architecture Award, in 1998 and 2000, and he also received the Tepe Centre Architectural Award in 2000 for two of his projects. He has never left the academic sphere, teaching at various schools of architecture and recently joining the faculty of Bilgi University to help start the first graduate school of architecture in the country.

Despite Tümertekin's deep immersion in Turkish architectural discourse and engagement with the professional and academic establishments of his city, his work cannot be easily placed in a local lineage. It does not even fit comfortably in the contemporary scene of younger Turkish architects with whom he frequently collaborates. Like the city's skyline, Istanbul's architecture is overwhelmed by the shadow of its Byzantine and Ottoman heritage and by postwar architects, most prominently Sedat Hakkı Eldem. Architectural production in the past twenty years has consistently failed to live up to the impressive heritage and also to the cosmopolitanism of Istanbul and, more recently, to the radicalization of lifestyles in the city.[2] Against an academically rich inquiry into the architectural and urban problems of the country, the architectural output has lacked luster in comparison. This is not to say that there was no significant architectural output in Istanbul during this period, but rather that the strong architectural culture has maintained most formal explo-

rations within the bounds of rather predictable debates about the role of modernism in building a nationalist identity. Even during the 1980s, when influential postmodern evocations opened up references outside the modernist palette, the discussion remained largely confined to the search for a national identity. And although a new generation of Turkish architects have become aggressively well versed in contemporary architectural forms and have contributed to architectural debates throughout the world, they have tended to ignore the continuity of these discussions with local academic debates and with practice, with the idea of context in general. Tümertekin's importance in this respect lies in his ability to transgress contextual arguments while maintaining an active interest in the conditions of practice and construction in Turkey.[3]

This transgression of context runs consistently throughout the work of Tümertekin, whether in his suburban residential developments, monuments, houses, or adaptive reuse projects, be they in Turkey, the Netherlands, or Japan, and even in the publications that his office sponsors, whether on Ottoman architecture or contemporary formal concepts. His incisive treatment of the site neither celebrates its idiosyncrasies expressionistically nor ignores them. In the Çatalhöyük Archeological Museum in Konya, for example, he creates both the site and the building by introducing a dent into the flatness of the terrain, but then complements it with a curved floating roof. Similarly, the B2 House carves a terrace in the sloping landscape, but then places a detached box on it. This double operation of marking and then erasing allows him to propose new contexts by carefully transgressing the original context.

The surgical approach to site through form is also extended to program, to the interior. Most of his buildings are treated as empty shells, the program shelved into closets or embedded in the thickness of walls. That is not to say that he is more concerned with volumes than their functions, but rather that he is interested in the tension that emerges between the possibility of activity and the empty space that contains it. The emptiness becomes the expressive means by which the established relationship between form and program is constantly interrogated. The idea of removal, or subtraction, as is evident in his introductory statement here, is central to his design approach.

For example, the Shibuya Friendship Monument in Japan is, at first blush, a satisfactory emblem of the modern-local dialogue, with fair-faced concrete on the exterior and Iznik tiles on the interior. Such a juxtaposition of materials would satisfy all that has been said about critical regionalism. Yet upon further examination, the isolation and privacy of the experience of the monument and the element of surprise through which the decorative aspect of the monument is presented to the viewer, as if the wrapping is inside the gift, makes the monument much more of a personal, rather than a cultural, gesture.

This approach would have been interpreted as a variation on contemporary apathy to context had it not been coupled with Tümertekin's immersion in the conditions of professional practice. The Optimum project presents a serious alternative to the themed and gated communities that are sprouting up everywhere in the Istanbul suburbs. Resorts such as the trend-setting Kemer Country are being built by American architects (usually from Florida) in a Mediterranean architectural style twice removed from its ostensible source—that is, a Spanish colonial style from Florida that gets reapplied to the other end of the Mediterranean, without the slightest sense of irony. The successful experiences of Sedat Hakkı Eldem in working with large-scale developers on gated communities may have gone unrepeated particularly because of the lack of respect developers tend to have for local architects' ability to produce market-oriented work.[4] In that regard, the Optimum project is an important breakthrough in terms of proposing a model for collaboration between architects and commercial developers and in bringing architecture to bear on a prevalent building and urban type. Tümertekin has displayed an ability to engage the real-estate dimension of the profession—not because of his willingness to compromise but to the contrary, because of his conviction that architecture has to constantly interrogate the possible in order to innovate. This project abounds in layout innovations, from the relationship between the houses and the club, to the relationships among the units, to the way in which the commercially driven flexibility of the unit is transformed into architectural openness.

Tümertekin's embrace of practice extends from patronage issues to those of construction. Another characteristic approach in his work is the generative strength of the detail, of one particular detail in every project. Frequently, the most telling drawing is the section detail, where the close-up view of the construction logic is extended into a perspectival view of the space of the building, showing the relationship between the detail and the enclosure that it generates. Invariably, the detail is primarily the shell (whether in SM House or the Shibuya Monument). The

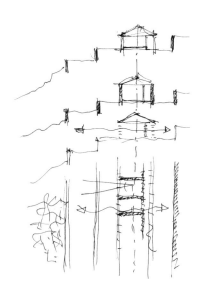

details often appear at first to be fairly standard, but a slight twist to one aspect of the construction logic generates the novelty in the project and its expression. The rotation of the stone in the façade of B2 House and the stone wrapping over the glass roof in the SM House are two such examples.

What is unique about this material innovation is how obvious—almost necessary—it seems, and yet how it helps us rethink some major disciplinary parameters of materials and spaces. This interrogation of the discipline extends to the techniques of representation as well. Tümertekin sometimes conflates the construction drawing with the representation of his architecture, emphasizing the continuity between construction and its effects. The plan drawing is mostly a perimeter outline, the compositional possibilities of plan reduced to the articulation of the thickness of the enclosure. Generally the drawings are very direct, as if making denotations rather than representations, almost untainted by the allographic attributes of architectural drawing, as if here again deferring expression to construction.

In the recent work of Han Tümertekin, every project is an encounter between materials, professional skills rooted in the design problem and its peculiarities, and contingencies—only to take these aspects to a level of resolution and formal abstraction that enters in a dialogue with contemporary architecture at large. Every encounter is an opportunity for reinventing both context and architecture, a condition that philosopher Kwame Anthony Appiah has described as "rooted cosmopolitanism." This strategic strangeness in the world is needed to maintain the uniqueness of experience.[5] This strangeness to the Turkish context allows Tümertekin to propose challenging changes to the way that an architect can practice, by grounding himself in the circumstances of building in order to change them, without being bogged down by the cultural debates that have confined architecture to a narrow range of expressive possibilities.

When asked about the problem of identity in contemporary architecture at a recent conference in Istanbul, Han Tümertekin elegantly turned the question around to point to his own identity.[6] He argued that it was not so much the identity of the nation-state or the culture that was at stake but his identity as an architect; this identity is formed by his education, his concerns, but also what makes it to the design table in his office in terms of immediate building- and construction-related issues. In other words, he distinguishes between the uniqueness-of-character aspect of identity and the notion of identification or belonging. In doing so, he also asserts that the link between them is culturally determined. While constructing his own identity as an architect, he can help elucidate the question of national identity. Architectural identity as conceived by Tümertekin, like other identities, is constructed, but perhaps more than other formal symbols or presence, it can expose and explain the artifice.

Notes

1. For further documentation of these projects, see *Architecture for a Changing World*, exhibition catalog of The Aga Khan Awards for Architecture, 1980–1998, held at the Fundacion Internacional de Sintesis Arquitectonica (Seville: FISA, 1999).

2. For a good description of Istanbul's recent social history, see Andrew Mango, *The Turks Today* (Woodstock and New York: Overlook Press, 2004).

3. For an insightful and concise survey of modernism and nationalism in Turkish architecture, see Sibel Bozdogan, "The Predicament of Modernism in Turkish Architectural Culture: An Overview," in Sibel Bozdogan and Reşat Kasaba, eds., *Rethinking Modernity and National Identity in Turkey* (Seattle and London: University of Washington Press, 1997), 133–156.

4. This sentiment was conveyed to me by several established real estate developers in Istanbul.

5. Kwame Anthony Appiah, *The Ethics of Identity* (Princeton and Oxford: Princeton University Press, 2005).

6. Conference on the Aga Khan Awards held at the Istanbul Technical University in November 2005.

SUBTRACTION *Han Tümertekin*

The most remarkable architectural observation I have is not about a building but about two people playing backgammon. As a student of architecture, I encountered a scene that fundamentally shook my perception of space. Until that day, I thought that the only way to create space was to build, to add things to what already existed. The example that led me to rethink this idea reached a solution by subtracting; it created space not by filling but by emptying.

It is about two people playing backgammon. A very hot and sunny day. Noontime, the sun is directly above, shadows have shrunk. They are seated on low stools, facing each other, knees touching. Both just fit in the shadow cast by a sign. They are playing gaily, the board resting on their legs. Everything is fine. Real, mundane, simple, easy, and incredibly poignant.

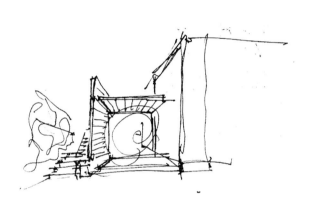

SM HOUSE

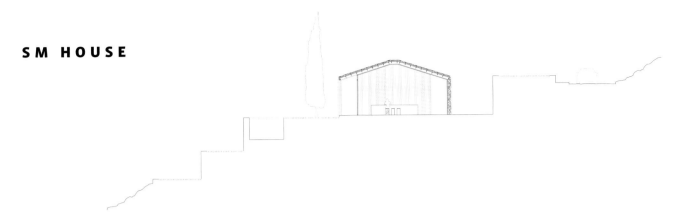

A-A section

This is a vacation house for a four-person family and their friends. The site is on the hilltop of an Aegean village, bordered by a road to the north. This is both a weekend and a guest house for multiple users. The covered house acts as a filter for the open house it accommodates in the front and back. Living space is syncopated by rooms. The main structural element of the house is the curtain wall that runs north-south, emphasizing the house's permeability. The outer shell of the house is supported by steel construction at 1.6-meter intervals. The stone wall that borders the north of the site continues along the ground, rises along the back of the house, and covers it on the roof. The view follows this wrap of stone.

TITLE
NAME OF WORK SM HOUSE
BUILDING TYPE SINGLE HOUSE

LOCATION
AREA AYVACIK, BÜYÜKHUSUN
CITY ÇANAKKALE
COUNTRY TURKEY

DATES
PROJECT 1997–2005
EXECUTION 2006

AREA
LOT 1,200 M2
PROJECT 400 M2

CLIENT
SEDEF-MURAT ÖZTÜRK

ARCHITECTURE
COMPANY MİMARLAR TASARIM LTD., ISTANBUL
ARCHITECT HAN TÜMERTEKİN
PROJECT ARCHITECT EYLEM ERDİNÇ

CONSULTANCY
CONSTRUCTION COMPANY SİSKA İNSAAT
LOCAL COORDINATOR ZIYA ILDIZ

STRUCTURE
COMPANY TEKTAS MÜHENDİSLİK
STRUCTURAL ENGINEER HAKAN ÇATALKAYA

View of the house with terraces

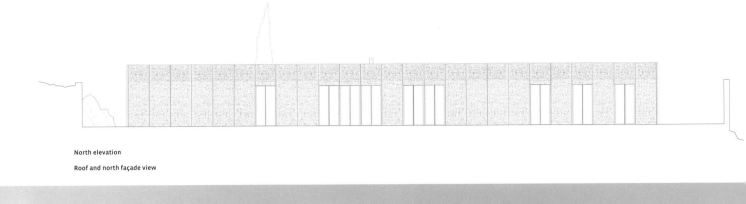

North elevation

Roof and north façade view

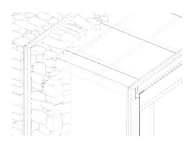

View of roof

Construction detail

View of wall detail

South façade view

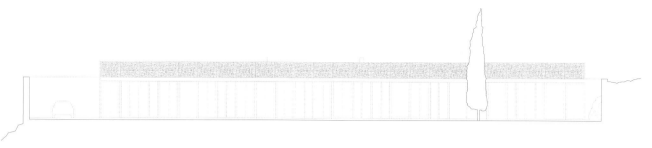

South elevation

View of roof detail

View from the courtyard

View from south patio

Interior view from the courtyard

Interior view from the living area

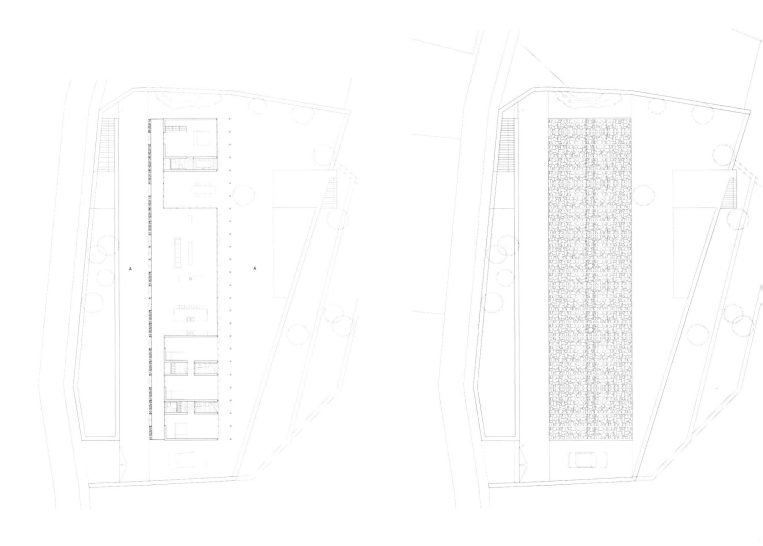

Plan

Site plan

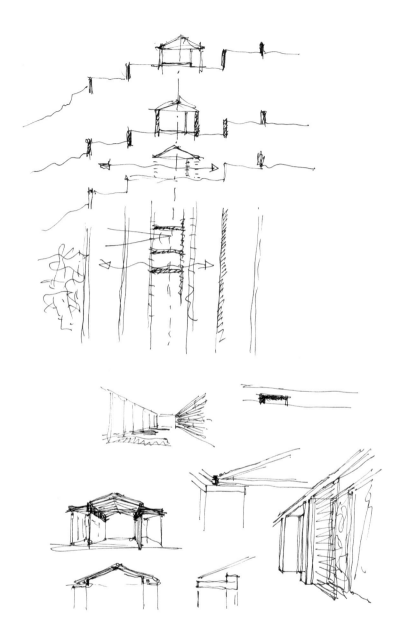

Study of terracing condition

B2 HOUSE

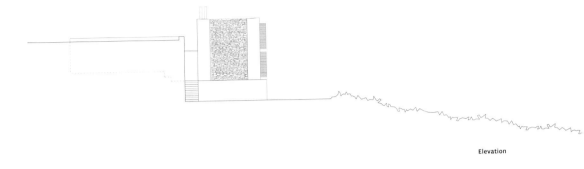

Elevation

View of the house from downhill

User: A contemporary nomad, changing places frequently, intensively using the latest information technologies and thus acting independent of "place," even in the house itself. How compulsory is it for a nomad's house to belong to its particular place, in this case near a hillside village, an olive grove, and the sea?

Criteria: Short-term use, low maintenance, locally made but non-native house.

Place: Ayvacik, an Aegean village.

Materials, structure, and construction: The main structure of the house is concrete. Other walls are hand-crafted stone. The balcony is steel construction with a wooden floor extending toward the interior. The ground floor is mosaic and natural stone. Window framing and shutters are low-maintenance aluminum. Aluminum shutters are filled with hand-crafted reed, enabling natural ventilation.

TITLE
NAME OF WORK B2 HOUSE
BUILDING TYPE SINGLE HOUSE

LOCATION
AREA AYVACIK, BÜYÜKHUSUN
CITY ÇANAKKALE
COUNTRY TURKEY

DATES
PROJECT 1999–2000
EXECUTION 1999–2000

AREA
LOT 600-M2
PROJECT
150 M2

CLIENT
SELMAN BİLAL, SÜHA BİLAL

ARCHITECTURE
COMPANY MIMARLAR TASARIM LTD., ISTANBUL
ARCHITECT HAN TÜMERTEKIN
PROJECT ARCHITECT EYLEM ERDİNÇ
ASSISTANT ARCHITECTS HAYRIYE SÖZEN,
AHMET ÖNDER

LOCAL CONSULTANCY
PROJECT COORDINATOR ZİYA ILDIZ
STRUCTURE COMPANY PARLAR MÜHENDİSLİK
STRUCTURAL ENGINEER GÜLSÜN PARLAR
PHOTOGRAPHY CEMAL EMDEN

AWARDS
2000 TEPE ARCHITECTURAL CULTURE CENTRE AWARDS
2004 AGA KHAN AWARD FOR ARCHITECTURE

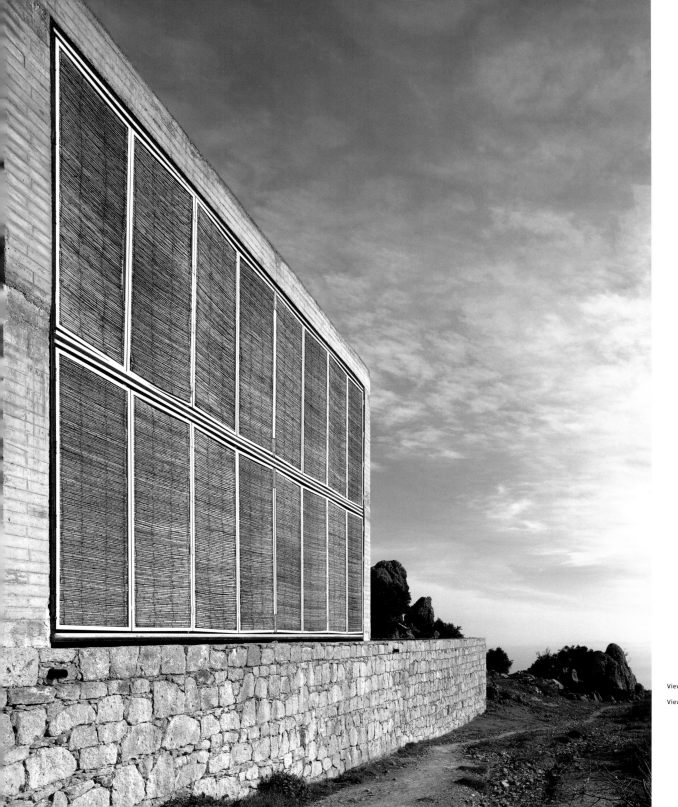

View of south façade with closed sh[u...]
View of south façade with opened sh[...]

First-floor front façade and interior detail

View from ground-floor interior

View of the house overlooking the sea

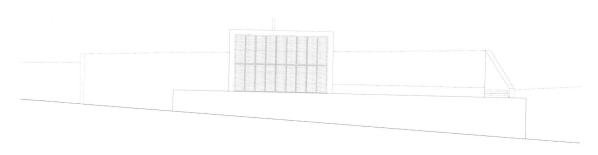

Front elevation

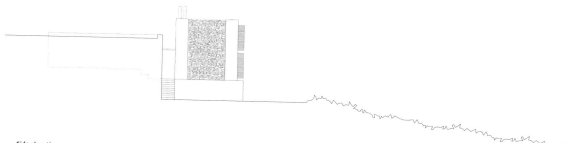

Side elevation

Section

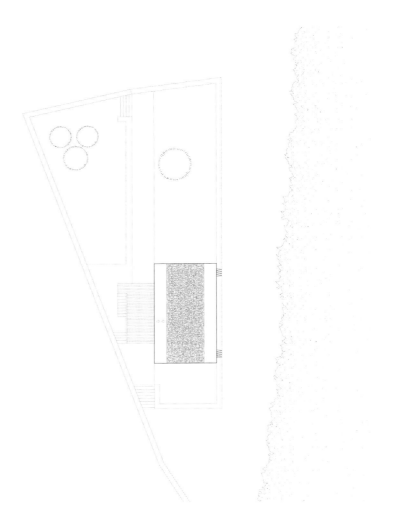

Site plan

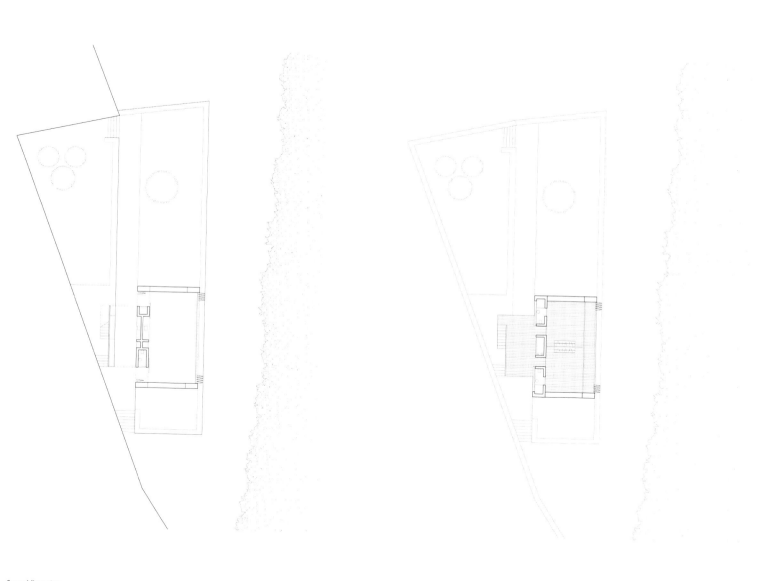

Ground-floor plan

First-floor plan

OPTIMUM

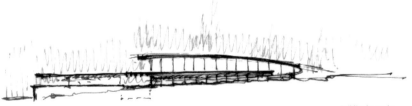

Building lot study

The Optimum housing development is composed of eighty-four houses of four types. The houses are bordered by the former Sile road and the forest. Each building lot is a different size and shape, and the houses' entrances and orientations vary. Each house is modified to fit its immediate surroundings without a front or a back. The houses have three components surrounded by a garden: living room, dining room, kitchen, and master bedroom on the upper level; garage, storage, maid's room, home office, and kids' room on the ground level; and space that accommodates different entrance and circulation options. The houses are differentiated by the rooms being closer together or farther apart. Although situated under one roof, different spaces for parents and children can be regarded as two separate houses. Both areas face the two-story space that looks out on the view. When going from one room to the next or from one floor to another, one passes through this two-story volume, making each displacement an architectural promenade within the interior spaces. This continuity carries through to the relation with the exterior.

TITLE
NAME OF WORK OPTIMUM HOUSING

LOCATION
AREA ÖMERLİ
CITY ISTANBUL
COUNTRY TURKEY

DATES
PROJECT 1999
EXECUTION 2000–2003

AREA
LOT 80,000 M2
PROJECT 24,000 M2

CLIENT
TUBASIM

ARCHITECTURE
COMPANY MIMARLAR TASARIM LTD., ISTANBUL
ARCHITECT HAN TÜMERTEKIN
PROJECT TEAM HAYRİYE SÖZEN, AHMET ÖNDER, EYLEM ERDINÇ
PROJECT COORDINATOR HALUK ONAY

CONSULTANCY
CONSTRUCTION COMPANY MTA BDK
STRUCTURE COMPANY PARLAR MÜHENDİSLİK
STRUCTURAL ENGINEER GÜLSÜN PARLAR
ELECTRIC COMPANY HB TEKNIK
INTERIOR DESIGN ARCHITECT MIMARLAR TASARIM
LANDSCAPE COMPANY CARKA
MECHANIC COMPANY TANRIOVER MÜHENDİSLİK
MODELS COMPANY SAYISAL DÜSLER

View of the covered tennis court

Site plan

Aerial view

Objective The development process of Optimum began with a thorough analysis of the current situation of land development in Turkey and worldwide. It was decided that Optimum would respond to contemporary issues in architecture in the world today, not only to problems of Muslim or developing countries. The design would not be a replica of a western approach, nor would it force localized solutions onto the process.

Optimum would not be an architectural show: it would be need-based, not pretentious; bold, not conformist; honest, not fake; plain and clear-cut, not ornamental. One objective is to show that good design is not expensive; on the contrary, it reduces costs. The major objective is to change and even redefine suburban living in a developing country, setting an example. In

Ground-floor plan, first-floor plan, I-I section, II-II section

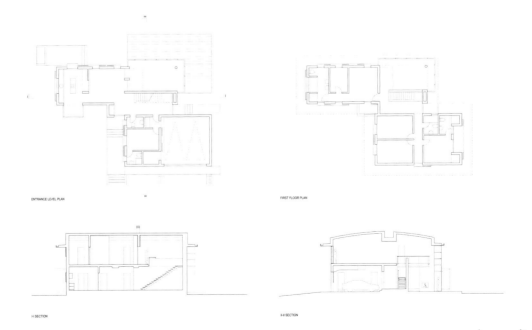

ENTRANCE LEVEL PLAN

FIRST FLOOR PLAN

I-I SECTION

II-II SECTION

0   5m

this respect, Optimum is a case study and a first step from which various extensions will be explored in the years to come. Inevitably, this first step is geared toward the middle class; it is difficult to compete with the makeshift, unofficial housing that now serves low-income residents. As these kinds of projects become more common, however, there will be a move toward accommodating lower-income groups, allowing a large number of people to benefit from the Optimum design philosophy.

Concept Optimum does not borrow foreign architects or architectural approaches, for that matter. It does, however, use contemporary architectural formation in the world as well as in the region. Similarly, instead of using the popular method of modernizing the classical Turkish house, a

Ground-floor plan, first-floor plan, I-I section, II-II section

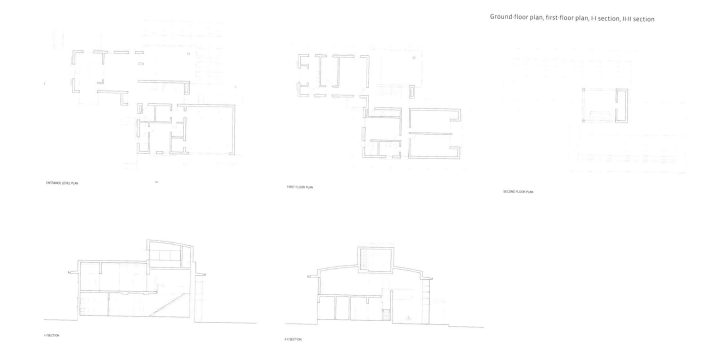

ENTRANCE LEVEL PLAN

FIRST FLOOR PLAN

SECOND FLOOR PLAN

I-I SECTION

II-II SECTION

fresh approach is pursued. The methodology is to answer each question as it arises, applying design solutions to localized problems with global as well as local tools, thus optimizing cost effectiveness and quality. This involves avoiding forced modern materials, construction techniques, or architectural approaches.

As such, Optimum is a bold and innovative project that does not imitate previous approaches, instead starting from its own point zero. Emphasis is placed on the process, not the final product. The process consists of concept development, land acquisition, administrative procedures, finance, conceptual program, architectural program, architectural design, engineering design, construction, marketing, sales, maintenance, and public relations. This requires coordinated teamwork and an integrated approach, taking infrastructure, recreation areas, landscape, and residential areas into consideration.

Solution One major dilemma is the distinction between the concepts of housing for the masses versus customized solutions. The approach taken here is to develop a typology to generalize the design. The commonly used theme-oriented development is replaced by concept development and solution-seeking design.

There are a number of specific design goals: providing independence to users, yet still allowing them to spend time together through spatial organization and effective sound insulation; integrating inner/outer living through spatial organization; focusing on architectural solutions that facilitate an experience of nature for those living in the house; and applying specialized orientation and spatial design, taking wind and sun orientation into account. The developer-architect relationship has been of utmost importance to the process, allowing freedom for the architect yet upholding the objective criteria.

Result Various objective criteria can be used to measure the degree of success that Optimum has enjoyed. First, sales figures have been very good in a period when the local economy was going through a depression. Second, there are already imitations on the market. More important, the general approach has started to be adopted by other projects. Third, positive responses from clients, the media, and the professional, industrial, finance, and intellectual communities show that a favorable public perception has been established, beyond the target group. Fourth, there have been thousands of communications from the public, asking when this approach will be available for lower-income citizens. This widespread interest suggests that the original intention of making this approach available to a large number of people is indeed not too far away; the crucial first step has been taken.

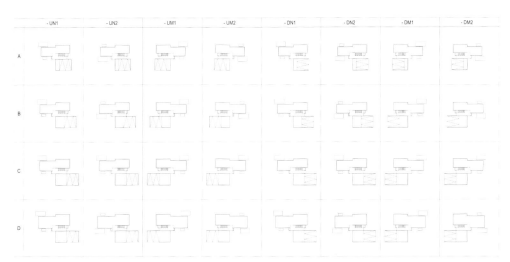

	- UN1	- UN2	- UM1	- UM2	- DN1	- DN2	- DM1	- DM2
A								
B								
C								
D								

Plan and section typologies

Interior view of the living area with double-height volume

View of the sports complex in the central park

View of th

View of the swimming pool overlooking the covered tennis court

Building lot studies

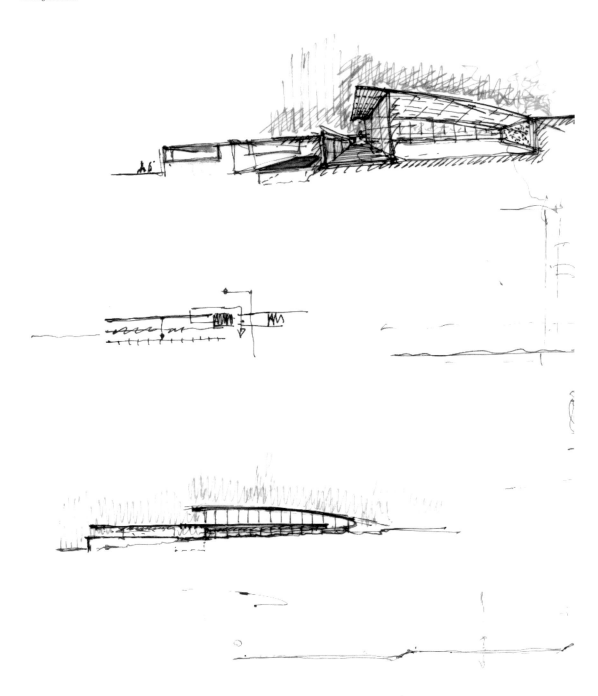

THE ECONOMY BANK N.V. (TEBNV)

This is a bank headquarters building in Amsterdam. The site is in the Amstelveen area, the location of many multinational companies. The site is surrounded by a canal to the west and a road to the east. The prismatic structure is composed of two parts. The main entrance façade is a massive crust. Behind it, the transparent office space that faces the canal allows changes in use. The building redefines the land-water line and the offices are situated over the water. The transparency behind is traced on the front façade by the vertical bands of windows. These traces continue on the landscape between the building and the road.

North elevation sketch

View from main entrance

TITLE
NAME OF WORK THE ECONOMY BANK N.V. (TEBNV)
BUILDING TYPE OFFICE

LOCATION
AREA KRONENBURG, AMSTELVEEN
CITY AMSTERDAM
COUNTRY NETHERLANDS

DATES
PROJECT 2001–2002
EXECUTION 2004

AREA
LOT 3,000M2
PROJECT 2,000M2

CLIENT THE ECONOMY BANK N.V. (TEBNV)

ARCHITECTURE
COMPANY MIMARLAR TASARIM LTD., ISTANBUL
ARCHITECT HAN TÜMERTEKIN
PROJECT ARCHITECT EYLEM ERDINÇ
LOCAL ARCHITECTURE COMPANY ZZDP ARCHITECTEN, AMSTELVEEN
PROJECT COORDINATOR ROB DUINDAM

CONSULTANCY
CONSTRUCTION COMPANY SLAVENBURGH'S BOUWBEDRIJVEN B.V. (SBB)
PROJECT COORDINATOR JOS VIESELMAN
CONSULTANCY COMPANY VAN GOOL AND PARTNERS B.V.
PROJECT COORDINATOR HANS GOSEWEHR
STRUCTURE COMPANY TECHNISCH BUREAU C.DE HEER B.V.
STRUCTURAL ENGINEER COR DE HEER
QUALITY SURVEYOR COMPANY KATS AND WAALWIJK B.V.
PROJECT COORDINATOR URBAN C.J.VAN DER MADE

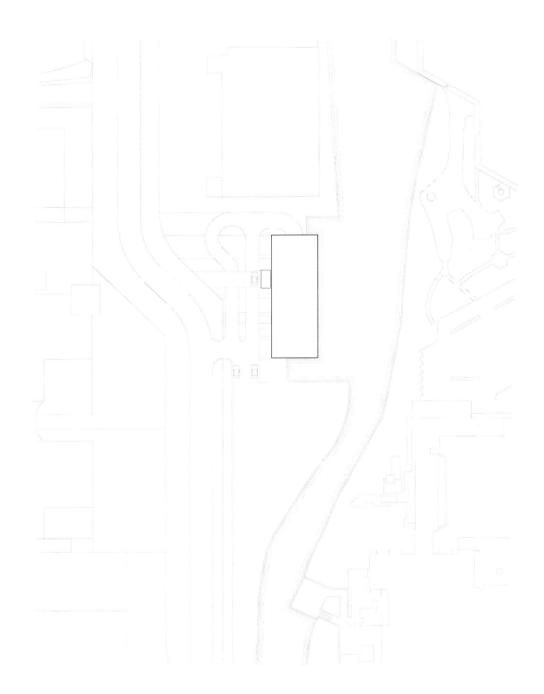

Site plan

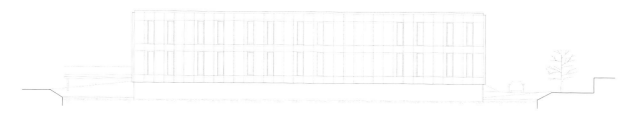

North elevation

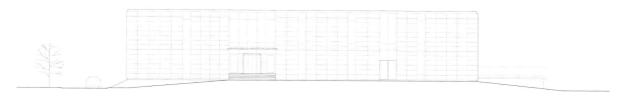

South elevation

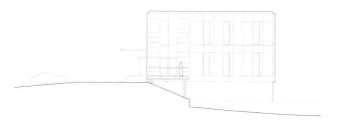

East elevation

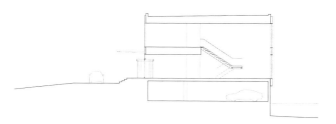

AA section

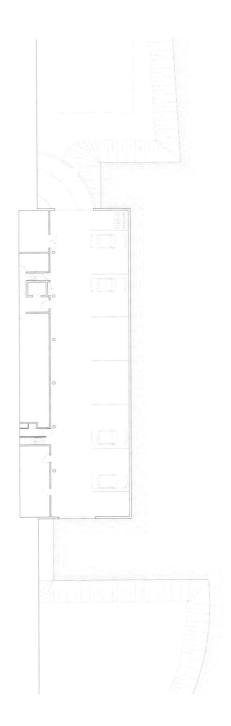

Basement plan

Ground-floor plan

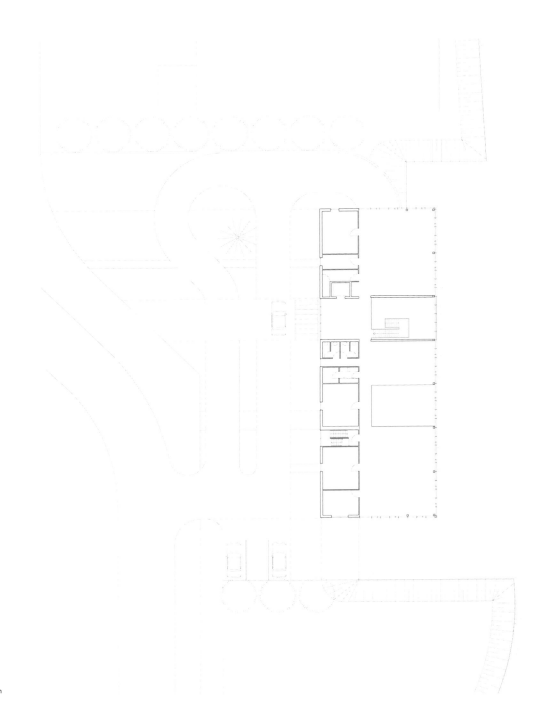

First-floor plan

South façade overlooking the river

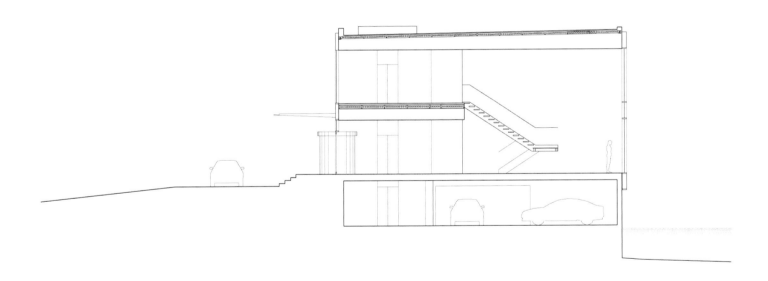

Section

Interior view from the entrance hall overlooking the river

SHIBUYA MONUMENT

The Turkish-Japan Friendship Monument was built to commemorate the designation of 2003 as the "Year of Turkey" in Japan. The 2-meter-wide, 4-meter-high monument is located in a vibrant Tokyo square that features large audiovisual communication devices overlooking City Hall. The monument is about creating an introverted space that could be distinguished from a distance, but not consumed.

Because Shibuya Square accommodates underground parking, the location, size, and weight of the monument is specified by Japan Construction and earthquake codes. Another determining condition is the use of tulip-printed Iznik tiles as a recognized symbol of Turkish culture. The wall is made of four precast carbon-fiber reinforced concrete pieces and is covered with Iznik tiles inside.

The wall is created to hold the tiles and coiled to surround the visitor. One enters the exposed concrete cylinder through a cut, perhaps for a moment of silence or reflection.

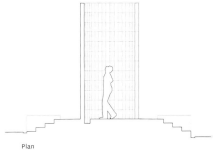

Plan

North view of the monument in front of City Hall

TITLE	DATES	CLIENT	CONSULTANCY
NAME OF WORK SHIBUYA MONUMENT	**PROJECT** 2002 **EXECUTION** 2003	MINISTRY OF FOREIGN AFFAIRS, TURKISH REPUBLIC	**CONSTRUCTION COMPANY** KAJIMA CO. **PROJECT COORDINATOR** HAN TÜMERTEKİN **ELECTRIC COMPANY** ERCO
LOCATION **AREA** SHIBUYA **CITY** TOKYO **COUNTRY** JAPAN	**AREA** **LOT** 5M2 **PROJECT** 5M2	**ARCHITECTURE** **COMPANY** MİMARLAR TASARIM LTD., ISTANBUL **ARCHITECT** HAN TÜMERTEKİN	

Opposite: Interior view of monument's
wall covered with Iznik tiles

Iznik tile detail

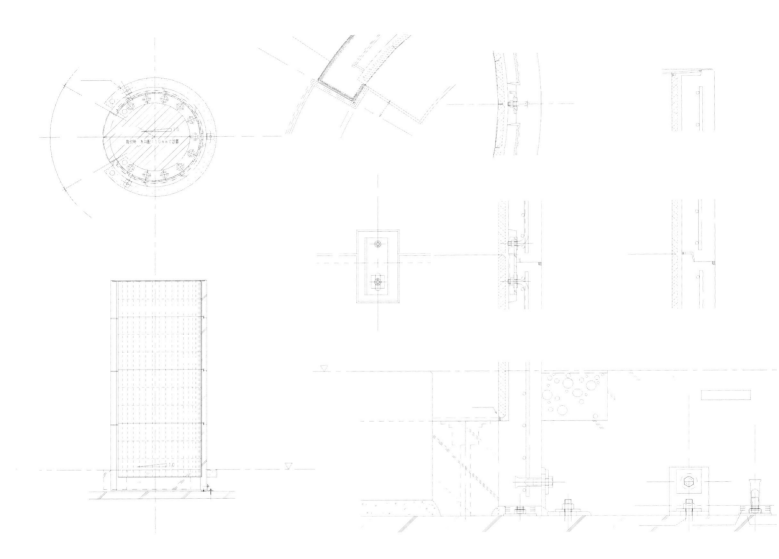

Construction details

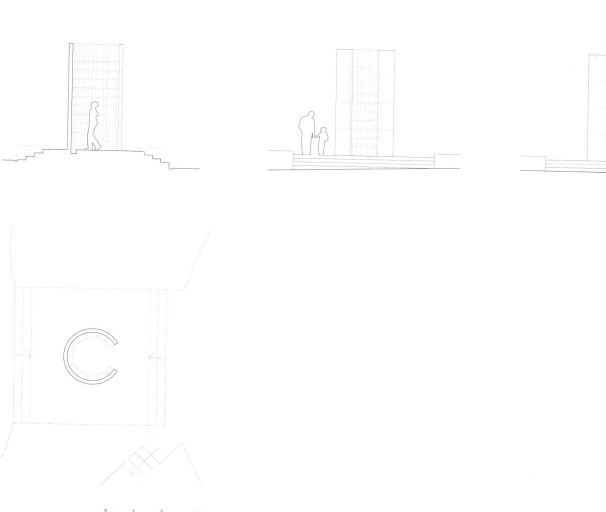

Plan, section, North elevation, South elevation

CONTRIBUTORS

HAN TÜMERTEKİN

Han Tümertekin is a practicing architect based in Istanbul. He worked as an architect in Paris before establishing Mimarlar Tasarım in 1986. Since then, he has been involved in residential, commercial, and institutional projects both in Turkey and abroad. Tümertekin received a Bachelor of Architecture degree from Istanbul Technical University (1986), and he completed graduate studies in Historic Preservation at Istanbul University (1988). Besides heading a professional practice, he has taught at many universities; he is currently teaching at the Harvard University Graduate School of Design. He also lectures at major universities and cultural institutions including TU Delft, MAAN (Tokyo), and Days of Oris (Zagreb). His completed projects have achieved high visibility in the architecture/design world. Publications include: *Domus, World Atlas of ContemporaryArchitecture, Abitare,* and *AV Monografias.* He was awarded the Aga Khan award for the B2 House. His recent work was exhibited in the Venice Biennale 2006.

NEYRAN TURAN

Neyran Turan is an architect and a doctoral candidate at the Harvard University Graduate School of Design. She received a B.Arch. degree from Istanbul Technical University and holds a masters degree from Yale University's School of Architecture. Turan has taught at the GSD, Yale, Boston Architecture College, and Istanbul Technical University. Turan's work explores urbanism and global networks in contemporary culture. Her recent publications include contributions to *Thresholds, ACSA Surfacing Urbanisms,* and *Landscapes of Development.* Turan is currently acting as the publications coordinator for the GSD's Aga Khan Program.

RENGIN TOROS

Rengin Toros is a practicing architect based in Istanbul. She completed undergraduate studies at Istanbul Technical University and was awarded a Fulbright Scholarship to attend Columbia University's Graduate School of Architecture. Later she worked at Lot-Ek and Skidmore, Owings, and Merrill. She joined Mimarlar Tasarım in 2005.